PURPOSED
TO
PROSPER

5 Principles To Master In Order To Master Money

Kirstie O'Banner
Foreword by Samuel O'Banner

Purposed To Prosper
5 Principles to Master In Order To Master Money

© 2025 by Kirstie O'Banner

ISBN:979-8-218-80683-5

Cover design by Aslan; Exterior/Interior Photo by Tavis Porter; Book/Editing Services by Sonquenetta Collins

This book is dedicated
to Legaci.

I once heard someone say, "*What you learned late,
teach your children early*".
I'm so thankful to have learned these principles and
that I'll be able to not only teach them to you early,
but to model what walking in financial freedom and
obedience to the Lord looks like. I want you to know
what it means to trust God in every area of your life.
If you learn nothing else from me, may you learn this.
I love you.

Contents

Foreword

When my wife and I first began teaching and living out the principles in this book, our initial desire was to begin to seek God's way of handling money as outlined in the scriptures. What started as simple habits—tracking our spending, setting goals, saying "no" when the world said "yes"—quickly became a framework that reshaped our family tree.

We've paid off debt, built savings, invested wisely, and most importantly, gained the peace of mind that comes from knowing we are in control of our finances, not the other way around. These pages hold more than advice; they hold the roadmap we used to change our financial future.

I'll be honest—what you're about to read goes against the grain of modern culture. We live in a world that encourages instant gratification, glorifies lifestyle inflation, and measures success by what's visible on the outside. But the truth is, building real, lasting wealth often means doing the opposite of what's popular. It means sacrifice, discipline, and intentionality. It means choosing contentment over comparison. This book is an invitation to reject the pressure to keep up and instead, build a life of freedom and purpose—on your terms.

If you commit to these principles, like we did, you won't just change your bank account—you'll change your legacy. That's the power of what's in your hands right now. Read it with an open mind and a willing heart. Your future self—and your family—will thank you.

Samuel O'Banner

Introduction

Well, hello there! I'm so glad you're here. Whether this is your first time reading a book on finance or you've tried to learn how to handle money wisely before, this book was written with YOU in mind!

This isn't just any book...this book is filled with timeless, divine wisdom taken directly from the pages of THE BOOK!!! You guessed it, THE BIBLE!

While I hope and pray that this book helps you understand biblical financial principles, the highest aim for this resource is to point you to the One who so graciously gave us the blueprint for handling money thousands of years ago and is still watching over His word to perform everything He promised.

Purposed to Prosper isn't just a catchy book title.
It's an incredible truth to be embraced by those who believe what the Bible says. YOU were purposed to prosper!! God intended for us (those who would follow His instructions on how to handle money) to live lives free from financial bondage and the stress that comes along with that. THIS, my friends, is how I define what it means to prosper!

No, it doesn't mean that everyone is going to be billionaires or even millionaires, but it does mean that financial security and freedom from the enslaving nature of mismanaged money is not only possible, but very much within reach for anyone who would take God at His word in this area!

The famous verse that inspired the title can be found in the book of Jeremiah - chapter 29, verse 11. It reads "For I know the plans I have for you," declares the Lord, "plans to prosper you and not to harm you, plans to give you hope and a future." The language God chose here should excite you! It indicates that God, the creator of the universe, made a plan for YOU! And not just any plan; a plan for you to PROSPER! A plan to give you HOPE and a FUTURE!

Not only does He have a plan for you, but He didn't leave it up to us to figure out the details of the plan or how to make the plan work for us. Instead, He so graciously gave us over 2,000 verses of scripture about money and possessions to help us navigate this topic that touches nearly every aspect of our lives.

The Bible is filled with financial principles that transcend cultural trends, economic cycles and centuries of an ever-changing world. We should pause here to define the word principle.

I like to say a principle is a transferable truth. Meaning if it's true for me, it's also true for you. And it would be true for anyone who applies it, whether they subscribe to the Christian faith or not.

In fact, these principles have been adopted by people from all over the world, from varying religions, for generations. Why? Because they work!! And they will work for anyone who is wise enough to put them into practice.

This book is written to help you understand and apply these principles in a practical and purposeful manner. And not just for this season of your life, but for the rest of your life!

My prayer for anyone reading this is that you will use it as a guide as you search the scriptures for yourself, trusting God to confirm to you what He wants you to take away from them and how to apply them to your life. I pray that you would approach it with an open heart and mind.

Be optimistic! Don't allow your mind to entertain reasons why this can't or won't work for you. I know those thoughts might come, but reject them and replace them with reasons why this can and will work for you.

The best reasons are that God is incapable of failing, His plans don't fail, and His word does not return void. Be confident in His purpose for you.

Trust that you, my friend, are PURPOSED TO PROSPER!

1
Stewardship

Before we discuss handling money, we must first define how to view money and possessions. Correcting our perspective on money may be the most impactful lesson in this book. Every other principle is built on the foundation of stewardship.

Most of us embrace the idea that our money is ours and it's up to us to manage it as we see fit. I mean, we go to work and earn a paycheck, so the money is ours, right?? WRONG!! Psalm 24:1 declares, "The earth is the Lord's, and everything in it, the world, and all who live in it.". This means what we have does not actually belong to us. We are not owners, but stewards (or managers) entrusted with resources that ultimately belong to God. Seriously ponder that for a moment. The implications of this truth are far too great to rush past. If what we have actually belongs to God, then He is the One we should rely on to know how to manage it. Our primary financial literacy tool should be the Bible!

I find it helpful to share this whenever I have an opportunity to teach on stewardship: Imagine you owned a very large and extremely successful company that you worked hard to build from the ground up. Because your company is so large, you'd have to hire others to help you manage the day-to-day operations of your business, right?

You'd also have to instruct your managers on the best way to carry out their duties so that the company can continue to thrive, right? You would know exactly how things should be done, because you created the company, right? You would also expect your managers to follow your instructions when carrying out their duties on behalf of the company.

Now, what would you do if you hired a manager who made no attempts to understand your instructions and instead made up their own practices for handling YOUR resources based on what they felt was best?

What if this manager were responsible for the company suffering huge financial losses due to their unwillingness to follow your instructions?

What would you do if that same manager asked for raises and promotions every day?

Isn't that a wild scenario? Now, consider this: when we don't look to God for instruction on how to handle money, we become just like that manager—asking for more and more from God while ignoring His instructions on what to do with HIS resources. That's a pretty crazy comparison, right?

If we are to experience the kind of financial freedom that God has in mind for us, we must embrace our role as stewards. Stewardship is a beautiful privilege that we've been given. No matter how much He's entrusted to you in this season, seek His will on how to manage it.

Another aspect of stewardship to consider is that it's not limited to just money. God is concerned about how we manage every aspect of our lives. Next, we will briefly look at what I like to call

The 4 Ts of Stewardship:

#1. Stewardship of Time

Time is one of our most precious and limited resources. Ephesians 5:15-16 exhorts believers to "be very careful, then, how you live—not as unwise but as wise, making the most of every opportunity, because the days are evil." Every day is a gift from God, and how we spend our hours reflects what we truly value.
Practical stewardship of time can include prioritizing daily communion with God, setting aside time for family, ministry, rest, and avoiding wastefulness through laziness or distractions.
Time well stewarded leads to a life that has eternal impact.

#2. Stewardship of Talents

God has given each believer unique abilities and spiritual gifts. 1 Peter 4:10 reminds us, "Each of you should use whatever gift you have received to serve others, as faithful stewards of God's grace in its various forms."

Our skills, education, and experiences are not accidental —they are divinely orchestrated for the good of God's kingdom.

A faithful steward asks:

How can my abilities bless the Church and the world?

Am I developing my talents to their fullest potential?

Do I recognize my gifts as grace, not grounds for pride?

When we faithfully use our talents, God multiplies their impact

for His glory and for the good of His people.

#3. Stewardship of Treasure

Of course, the most talked about aspect of stewardship is money & possessions (which the Bible sometimes refers to as treasure).

As I mentioned in the introduction, Scripture contains over 2,000 verses on wealth, possessions, and money management. Why? Because money reveals the heart. Jesus said, "For where your treasure is, there your heart will be also" (Matthew 6:21).

True stewardship of treasure involves:
Recognizing God as the provider of all wealth.
Giving generously and cheerfully.
Living within one's means and avoiding debt.
Investing in eternal purposes rather than temporary indulgences and so much more. We will look at these more closely later on.

#4. Stewardship of Testimony

Finally, stewardship extends to our witness for Christ. Paul calls believers "ambassadors for Christ" (2 Corinthians 5:20). Our character, integrity, and conduct are resources God entrusts to us for His mission.

Faithful stewardship of testimony includes:

Living with honesty and integrity in business and relationships.
Sharing the gospel boldly and wisely.
Reflecting Christ's love in every interaction.

Our testimony is often the only Bible some people will ever read. When managed well, it points others toward Christ, and that's the best thing we could ever do for anyone!

Stewardship is not about restriction—it is about freedom and reward. Jesus' parable of the talents (Matthew 25:14-30) illustrates that those who are faithful with little will be entrusted with much.

Faithful stewards experience:

Deeper intimacy with God—trust grows as obedience deepens.
Greater provision—not always materially, but always spiritually.
Eternal reward—hearing the words, "Well done, good and faithful servant." I mean, can you even imagine God himself giving you this type of affirmation?? What a beautiful reward to look forward to!

Stewardship is a daily choice to live with open hands and surrendered hearts towards God. Recognizing that it ALL belongs to Him.

Practical Application

1) Do you feel like you are a faithful steward?
If not, what areas do you think God is calling you to
surrender to Him?

_____

_____

_____

_____

_____

_____

_____

_____

2) How would your financial decisions be impacted if
you began to view the things you have as a manager
versus an owner?

_____

_____

_____

_____

_____

_____

_____

_____

Encouragement

Make a habit of asking God for direction and instruction in every area of your life, even the areas that you feel like you have under control. He knows what's best for you, and if He desires for you to prosper, to give you hope and a future (as He declared in Jeremiah 29:11), then He will certainly answer such prayers!

Notes

2
Budget

One of the most important aspects of learning to master money is the principle of budgeting. Budgeting is simply having a written plan for money. John Maxwell said that a budget is simply telling your money where to go instead of wondering where it went. Can you relate to wondering where your money went? I remember prior to learning to budget, I'd get paid, and before I knew it, I'd be convinced that my money had been stolen because I had no idea where it went! I'd start to backtrack my spending, trying to figure out what happened to the money. It was so stressful! I had no idea that taking the time to create a plan would save me a lot of money and headaches.

Budgeting is a powerful practice that even the wealthiest people and most powerful organizations understand the necessity of. From governments to practically every successful entity, you can bet your bottom dollar that they rely on budgeting to allocate their resources. Imagine if the federal government simply collected our tax dollars without any plan for how they would be used. There would be no order, and it would eventually result in the complete collapse of society. Sadly, the same happens every day for many of us when we don't budget; there is no order, and we live in a constant state of financial chaos.

Proverbs 21:5 reminds us, "The plans of the diligent lead surely to abundance, but everyone who is hasty comes only to poverty." Here we see a few things that I have to point out:

#1 - We need to have a PLAN for our money (budget)

#2 - We need to be diligent in planning/budgeting

#3 - Consistent budgeting WILL lead to abundance

#4 - Neglecting to take the time to budget WILL lead to poverty

Whether you never learned the importance of budgeting or you just don't know how, you picked up the right book! Although we won't be able to cover everything, when it comes to budgeting, I am hopeful that the framework to follow will help you to understand how to start budgeting and that you'll build on it as you become more familiar with the process and experience how it will transform your finances.

Before we dive into how to create a successful budget, I must stress the importance of approaching this process (as well as every budget you'll ever prepare) prayerfully! If what we have belongs to God, we need to begin the planning process by seeking His wisdom and guidance on how to use it.

Deuteronomy 8:18 declares, "Remember the Lord your God, for it is He who gives you the ability to produce wealth." Think about it, if God is the one who gives the ability to produce wealth, then our first step in budgeting needs to be getting on the same page with Him in this area! So, pray for His help. He will respond!

There are many different formats used for budgeting. They can be done using apps, spreadsheets, or good old pen and paper. Determine which method is best for you. It might be a good idea to experiment with each one to see what you're comfortable with.

I use and recommend what's called a **zero-based budget**. It simply means you give every single dollar a job. Instead of leaving money unassigned, you allocate it until your income minus your expenses equals **$0**. And, don't be alarmed by the zero!! This doesn't mean you have nothing left; it means everything has been planned for, whether it's giving, saving, or spending. Every single dollar should have an assignment in a successful budget.

Proverbs 27:23 reminds us, "Be sure you know the condition of your flocks, give careful attention to your herds." In today's terms, that means carefully knowing where every dollar is going. A **zero-based budget** provides clarity and will help you develop financial discipline.

Your budget should be completed PRIOR to the start of the budget period and should be consistent with your pay frequency.

For example, if you are paid every week on Friday, you will have a WEEKLY budget period, and your budget should be prepared by **Thursday** of each week.

If you are married, create a single household budget that includes all income and expenses. It's also a good idea to have budget meetings to discuss income, expenses, plan for upcoming changes, and larger expenses. Budgeting TOGETHER forces you to work as a team and creates opportunities to communicate personal and family goals, plan for the future, and establish accountability.

If you are single, consider seeking accountability amongst friends or family who may already be familiar with budgeting and managing money wisely. If you don't know anyone who can help you with this, join my Facebook community and connect with others who have read or are reading this book and may also be looking for accountability partners. This will help you stay on track!

Step 1: List ALL Income
Include:
Salary or wages
Side hustles
Business income
Child support, pensions, or benefits
Write this number at the top of your budget. This is the pool of resources God has entrusted to you for this pay period.

Step 2: Prioritize Giving
Before anything else, prayerfully decide how much you will give.
This amount may vary from one budget period to another or remain a set amount. However you decide to give is up to you, just make sure to give!

Step 3: Cover Essential Expenses
Next, assign money to your necessities:
Housing (rent or mortgage)
Utilities (electricity, water, internet)
Transportation (gas, insurance, bus fare)
Food (include groceries, restaurant meals, school lunches etc.)
Basic healthcare

Step 4: Allocate for Financial Priorities
Once essentials are covered, assign dollars to:
Debt repayment (if applicable)
Emergency savings
Long-term savings or retirement

Step 5: Budget for Lifestyle Expenses
Now you can add categories like:
Entertainment
Subscriptions
Clothing
Travel or hobbies

Step 6: Adjust Until It Balances to Zero
Keep adjusting your numbers until:
Income − Expenses = **$0**

If you have extra money left, assign it to savings, debt payoff, or giving. If you're short, reduce lifestyle spending until everything balances.

Example:
Income: **$3,500**
Giving: **$350**
Essentials: **$2,050**
Debt repayment: **$500**
Savings: **$300**
Lifestyle: **$300**
Remaining balance: **$0**

Step 7: Track and Review
Track your actual spending against your budget.
At the end of the budget period, review your progress and make any necessary adjustments for the next period.

If this is your first time budgeting, be patient with yourself and the process. You might completely blow your budget a few times before you get the hang of it. That's okay!! Just keep going until it becomes second nature. It will get easier as you stay consistent.

Cash Envelope System
One of the best ways to stay on track once you've created your budget is to use the cash envelope system. It helps you avoid overspending in certain budget categories. I used this method when my husband and I first got married and I was learning to budget for the first time. It helped me stay organized, know what I was spending, and how much I had left to spend in different categories. I took my envelopes everywhere with me, and I was proud to whip them out when it was time to pay!

I recommend getting a complete cash envelope system that has labels and pockets - you can find them on my website **www.KirstieOBanner.com** on the "Resources" page. You can also use plain paper envelopes and write on them.

Here's How it Works:

1. Complete a zero-based budget BEFORE your budget period begins.

2. Identify which categories would be best paid with cash and label each envelope accordingly. (groceries, restaurant meals, clothing/personal items, nails/hair appointments, etc., were a few I used envelopes for)

3. Refer to your budget and write the amount of cash allocated for each category on the appropriate envelope.

4. Withdraw enough cash to fund each category and place the exact amount needed in each envelope.

5. Keep envelopes with you and ONLY use the cash in each envelope for spending in each category.

6. Evaluate the effectiveness of your budget and adjust for the next budget period if necessary.

Practical Application

1) Download a zero-based budgeting app. I like Dave Ramsey's EveryDollar app (there is a free version that works just fine). Create an account and draft a budget.

2) Download a budget worksheet from my website www.KirstieOBanner.com on the "Resources" page. Create a budget for an upcoming budget period.

3) Request to join my private Facebook group Purposed To Prosper Community- for more information on budgeting.

4) In what areas do you see the most opportunity to minimize expenses in your budget?

_____

_____

_____

_____

5) Identify your budget periods based on your pay frequency. When and where do you plan to complete your budget? If you don't make a plan for completing it, you probably won't.

_____

_____

_____

_____

Encouragement

Learning to budget might be uncomfortable. It may take some time to get the hang of it. Embrace the challenge. Ask questions. Stay consistent.
Pray for wisdom, understanding, and discipline. It is not always easy, but it is worth it! You won't regret learning to budget effectively.

Notes

3

Get Out of Debt

In 2015, my husband, Samuel, and I paid off over $50,000 of debt in our first year of marriage! A few years later, we paid off our 30-year mortgage in just under 3 years!! Since then, we've been able to focus on building wealth, radical generosity, and enjoying a life of financial freedom!

When people hear our story, they often ask the same question...HOW?? I'd love to say that we are so brilliant that we came up with some groundbreaking financial hack that allowed us to pay off our debt and become millionaires, but the reality is that we chose to believe and obey God's word! That's it!

We have literally applied the same biblical financial principles that I lay out in this book. And just like they have worked for countless people from all walks of life for thousands of years, they worked for us too! Handling money God's way - getting out of debt, living below our means, giving generously, and investing wisely has absolutely changed our lives and our family tree.

Not only do we experience freedom in Christ, but we also gain freedom from the financial bondage that we had both become accustomed to before learning these principles. It wasn't an easy road to this type of freedom, but it was worth it, and I'd do it all over again if I had the chance!

I share some of my story to encourage and inspire you as we approach this chapter on getting out of debt.

As I mentioned, it's not an easy task. I won't sugarcoat it and make it seem like something you can do in your sleep. The road to debt freedom is one less traveled for a reason — it's hard! It's hard to say NO to the things we want in the moment. It's challenging to cut back on spending in areas that have become a part of your lifestyle. It's hard to live below your means and delay gratification.

Dave Ramsey says it this way - "Maturity is the ability to delay pleasure for a greater reward."

Getting out of debt requires maturity, discipline, and sacrifice. The good news is, you're not alone! You have our Heavenly Father on your side, ready to help you along the way. And trust me when I say this: when you commit to obey God's word and get out of debt, He will provide everything you need to see it through!

I couldn't even begin to describe all the divine happenings that we experienced while paying off debt. Unexpected checks arrived, along with promotions, career opportunities, and open door after open door! I believe He will show you the same kind of grace and favor as you embark on your journey to debt freedom!

As normal as the concept of borrowing and making debt payments may seem today, it is NOT how God intended for His people to live. Debt is one of the heaviest burdens a person can carry. It robs peace of mind, limits opportunities, and creates bondage that can last for years.

The Bible consistently warns against debt and offers wisdom on how God's people can live in a debt-free manner. While borrowing is not always condemned, Scripture reminds us that debt places us under obligation to others and should be avoided whenever possible.

Of course, Proverbs 22:7 comes to mind here -
"The rich rule over the poor, and the borrower is slave to the lender."

God does not want us enslaved to anything or anyone. Instead, He urges us to avoid borrowing and to pay it off quickly if we do find ourselves in debt.

Proverbs 6:1-4 says this: "...if you have trapped yourself by your agreement and are caught by what you said, follow my advice and save yourself, for you have placed yourself at your friend's mercy. Now swallow your pride; go and beg to have your name erased. Don't put it off; do it now! Don't rest until you do."

Wow! I remember the first time I read and understood this passage, my jaw dropped! God says here that if we have entered into an arrangement that puts us at the mercy of someone else (which is what owing someone money does), we should swallow our pride, beg to get out of it, do it immediately, and not rest until we have done so! Yikes!

Sounds like we need an attitude adjustment towards borrowing and getting out of debt. Most of us would take our time paying back money we've borrowed, often extending our repayment over years and years. That's years and years of not only being at the mercy of your creditor, but also years and years of paying thousands of dollars in interest.

Interest is the amount of money a creditor charges you for borrowing their money. Imagine if, instead of paying thousands of dollars in interest to someone else, you could earn thousands of dollars in interest on money that you invest wisely.

Earning versus paying interest is what I call being on the right side of the money matrix. This is where God wants His money, and He's entrusting us with getting it there!

STEPS TO GETTING OUT OF DEBT

#1 -Decide Against Debt

Before you begin to pay off debt, you must first decide that borrowing will no longer be an option for you. The Bible says that a wise man leaves an inheritance for his children's children. It's tough to build a financial legacy for the next generation when you're making debt payments and throwing away money paying interest each month.

Decide today that there's nothing you could buy that's worth your children's future. This shouldn't be just a temporary decision while you're getting out of debt; instead, make debt freedom a lifetime decision!

#2 - Emergency Fund

Next, you're going to establish an emergency fund. This is a specified amount of money that should be set aside for unexpected expenses while you're paying off debt. The emergency fund is essential to have in place because once you begin paying off debt, you're going to be throwing as much money as you can get your hands on towards those accounts, so it'll be wise to have money available to cover unexpected emergencies (i.e., flat tire, vehicle repair, appliance or home repair, etc.) should they arise.

#2 - Emergency Fund (continued)

The amount of your emergency fund will vary from person to person. For most people, I recommend a minimum of $2,000. If you feel more comfortable setting aside a little more, go for it! Just don't set aside too much, as that could slow down your progress with debt payoff.

A few things to note about the emergency fund and how to use it:

- Do not begin paying off debt until your emergency fund is in place.
- Keep it in a separate account so that you're not tempted to use it for non-emergencies.
- Be sure to immediately replenish your emergency fund if you use any portion of it. Pause debt payoff until you have restored your account to the $2,000 (or your designated amount).
- Only use for TRUE emergencies.

#3 - Debt Domino

In order to begin paying off debt, you have to first have a clear picture of how much you owe and who you owe it to. To figure this out, it might be helpful to pull your credit report and use it as a reference.

Once a year, www.annualcreditreport.com will allow you to print or download a free copy of your credit report from all three credit bureaus, Experian, Equifax, and TransUnion. Each report should provide the creditor's contact information and details for each account. Keep in mind that not all creditors report to the credit bureaus. You'll need to take your time and really think through ALL debt, even debt to family members or friends. Everything needs to be accounted for. Once you've gathered all your debts, you're going to list them in order from smallest to largest total amount owed. Include the name of the account, outstanding balance, minimum monthly payment, due date, and interest rate, if applicable.

Once this is done, you'll have what I like to call the DEBT DOMINO. You can download a copy of the Debt Domino worksheet from my website at www.KirstieOBanner.com, located on the "Resources" page.

Next, focus on aggressively paying off the smallest account first. You want to apply as much money as possible to this account each budget period. Meaning, after you have allocated funds for all of your essential expenses in your budget, designate as much as possible to that account. You're going to need to minimize our expenses in order to make real traction with accelerating debt payments. The more aggressive you are with freeing up funds, the faster you can get out of debt! I would strongly encourage you to find ways not only to minimize your expenses but also to generate additional income while paying off your debt.

You can find the "Minimizing Expenses Checklist" and the "Ideas for Increasing Your Income" downloads on my website, www.KirstieOBanner.com, on the "Resources" page.

Once you've paid off the smallest account on your Debt Domino, you're going to move on to the next one and repeat the process, taking the minimum payment you would have paid towards the previous debt and applying it towards the account that's up next. As you pay off the smaller accounts, you'll free up more funds to go towards the next account.

Remember, it's okay to celebrate along the way as you pay off accounts. But keep the celebrations inexpensive, as you keep your eyes on your ultimate goal. You will continue to aggressively accelerate debt payments until you become DEBT-FREE!

Practical Application

1) Calculate the total amount of debt you owe. Write the number on an index card and place it somewhere that you'll see it every day for motivation. How much debt do you owe, and where will you put your motivational reminder?

_____

_____

_____

2) How much will your emergency fund be? $2,000, or will you need more?

_____

_____

_____

3) After reviewing your credit reports, do you have any debt that you forgot about or weren't aware of?

_____

_____

_____

4) Which debt are you looking forward to paying off the most and why?

_____

_____

_____

Encouragement

Paying off debt is a tough yet rewarding process. If you ever start to feel like giving up, consider Psalm 37:21 - "The wicked borrow and do not repay, but the righteous give generously." Paying off debt is a matter of integrity. Take pride in keeping your word and paying what you owe. Your efforts and obedience to God's word will be rewarded!

Notes

4
Give
Generously

Generosity is by far my favorite topic to discuss. I can honestly say that the best part of financial freedom is not being able to buy nice things or travel around the world, but the ability to be generous — radically generous, even. My husband and I have experienced some of our greatest joy through giving to others. Our motivation for generosity is remembering how much has been given to us. The famous scripture John 3:16 is a beautiful reminder of just how much God loves us and what He was willing to GIVE as a result of that love. It reads "For God so loved the world that he gave his one and only Son, that whoever believes in Him shall not perish but have eternal life." Incredible, right? God GAVE His only son for us AND has promised to give those who believe in Him eternal life!

From Genesis to Revelation, the Bible reveals a generous God. Generosity is not just something God does; it's Who He is. As His children, we have opportunities to reflect His generous nature.
Biblical generosity isn't about giving because we have extra; it's about giving because we trust the God who has given us everything!

I always say generosity isn't something God wants FROM us, but it's something He wants FOR us! When Jesus said it is better to give than to receive, He meant it.

There are so many benefits to giving:

- Giving trains our hearts to serve God, not wealth.
- It realigns our priorities and keeps our spiritual vision clear.
- It defeats selfishness and materialism.
- It builds our faith as we trust God to meet our needs.
- It has eternal significance "...lay up for yourselves treasures in heaven..." — Matthew 6:20
- Guarantees our own continued blessing "A generous person will prosper; whoever refreshes others will be refreshed." — Proverbs 11:25

I could go on and on about why giving is good for us, but the primary motivation for our generosity should be simply because God said so! We see so many passages of scripture where God or Jesus admonishes us to give. And not only does He tell us to give, but He tells us how to give.

Consider the following:
Give Willingly
"Each of you should give what you have decided in your heart to give, not reluctantly or under compulsion..." 2 Corinthians 9:7
God cares about the heart behind the gift. Giving should be voluntary, joyful, and Spirit-led, not driven by guilt or fear.

Give Cheerfully

"...for God loves a cheerful giver." 2 Corinthians 9:7
Biblical generosity is marked by joy, not obligation. When we understand the impact of our giving and the eternal rewards that come with it, our hearts rejoice in the opportunity to give.

Give Sacrificially

"...she out of her poverty put in all she had to live on." Luke 21:4
Jesus praised the widow who gave just two small coins because her gift was costly. True generosity often requires sacrifice, not convenience.

Give Secretly

"But when you give to the needy, do not let your left hand know what your right hand is doing..." Matthew 6:3-4
God honors quiet, humble generosity. Public recognition isn't the goal; honoring God should be.

Practical Application

1) Is there anything that's keeping you from embracing a lifestyle of generosity? If so, what?

_____

_____

_____

2) What are some adjustments you can make in your current financial situation that will allow you to be more generous?

_____

_____

_____

3) Commit to a new act of generosity this week. Ask God for the faith and the resources to give like never before.

_____

_____

_____

Encouragement

The Bible is full of some incredible examples of generosity. Whether you are already a generous person or you're considering embracing a lifestyle of generosity, my prayer is that you would be an example to the rest of the world and live with an open hand and an open heart, always looking for ways to bless others; knowing that you can trust God with your needs as you are obedient to His instructions to give generously.

- "And my God will meet all your needs according to the riches of his glory in Christ Jesus."
— Philippians 4:19

Notes

5
Practice
Contentment

A few years ago, I read a book on contentment, which greatly helped me in this area. It opened my eyes to the fact that being content doesn't mean I shouldn't have desires or aspirations, but that I would live a life of constantly submitting those desires and aspirations to the Lord. Contentment isn't about not wanting anything; it's about wanting what God wants for us more than anything else. Exercising contentment demonstrates a willingness to rest in God's provision for you, knowing that it is what's best for you in that season.

I once heard someone describe contentment this way: To be content is to joyfully and quietly rest in God's provision for each day.

In every generation, people chase after more—more money, more possessions, more recognition, and more comfort. Yet, even with abundance, many still feel empty. The Bible presents a radical truth: true contentment does not come from what we have, but from who has us. The key is not the WHAT of your circumstances, but the WHO that has you in the palm of His hand!

The Apostle Paul declared, "I have learned to be content whatever the circumstances. I know what it is to be in need, and I know what it is to have plenty. I have learned the secret of being content in any and every situation... I can do all this through Him who gives me strength" (Philippians 4:11–13).

Contentment is not passive disinterest in what's going on in our lives, but an active choice to trust God, rest in His provision, and find joy in His will for us. It is a heart posture; cultivated through faith, gratitude, stewardship and experiencing the faithful nature of God as our Father. Contentment grows when we believe God will supply what we need, when we need it. The longer we walk with Him, the easier it becomes to trust not only His heart, but also His hand.

Now that we have looked into what contentment means, let's take a moment to identify why many of us struggle in this area.

Obstacles to Contentment

Comparison
Looking at what others have breeds envy and disrupts contentment.
Galatians 6:4-5 urges us to focus on our own walk with God instead of measuring ourselves against others.

Greed and Materialism
Jesus warned in Luke 12:15: "Watch out! Be on your guard against all kinds of greed; life does not consist in an abundance of possessions."

Ecclesiastes 5:10 reminds us, "Whoever loves money never has enough; whoever loves wealth is never satisfied with their income."

Fear of Lack
Worry about the future often robs today's joy. Matthew 6:31–33 teaches us to seek God's kingdom first, trusting Him to provide.

Entitlement
Feeling like we deserve or have earned things in life. Also, we often feel that we don't deserve certain realities, so we should be spared from them.

There are many more reasons people struggle with being content. Regardless of the cause, to live a life free from financial bondage and to truly prosper in this area, we should strive to be able to have a heart posture like that of the writer of Proverbs 30:8-9 – "Give me neither poverty nor riches; feed me with the food that is needful for me..."

Whenever I find myself feeling restless in my current situation or yearning for more than what I have, I try to recognize it as discontentment and begin to ask God for help.

Here are some of the ways I combat discontentment:

-Spending time reflecting on and thanking God for His provision.

-Removing social media and shopping apps from my phone for a season.

-Focusing on the needs of others.

-Giving away possessions.

Think and pray through these. The next time you find yourself lacking contentment, respond first by asking God for His help. He will give you a strategy that works for you.

If this is a consistent struggle for you, I'd encourage you to keep scriptures like Hebrews 13:5 before you (somewhere you'll see it every day or multiple times a day). It reads: "Keep your life free from love of money, and be content with what you have, for he has said, 'I will never leave you nor forsake you.'" What a beautiful and comforting reminder.... We can be confident that we will never go without what we need because our Heavenly Father has promised never to leave nor forsake us! And that's a promise we can take to the bank!

Practical Application

1) Can you relate to feeling discontent? In what areas do you struggle to be content?

_____

_____

_____

_____

2) What do you think contributes to your lack of contentment?

_____

_____

_____

_____

3) Ask God to help you rest in His provision for you. Remember, this does not mean that you cannot aspire to have more or achieve things; it simply means that you should always submit those desires to God and trust what He does/provides in your life.

Notes

Conclusion

We've explored five biblical principles that can transform your finances and enable you to prosper as God truly intended: stewardship, generosity, planning, eliminating debt, and living with contentment. These aren't just concepts to study; they're tools to transform the way you experience money and, ultimately, life. But let me be clear—the Bible has so much more to say about money & possessions.

A few other principles worth mentioning:
- Protecting your financial future by not co-signing: Proverbs 17:18 "It's poor judgment to guarantee another person's debt or put up security for a friend."

Proverbs 22:26-27 "Don't agree to guarantee another person's debt or put up security for someone else. If you can't pay it, even your bed will be snatched from under you."
- Building wealth through wise investing: Matthew 25:14 30 (Parable of the Talents): *"To those who use well what they are given, even more will be given, and they will have an abundance."* (v. 29) Ecclesiastes 11:2 *"Invest in seven ventures, yes, in eight; you do not know what disaster may come upon the land."* (diversification)

- teaching your children so they don't repeat the same mistakes:

Proverbs 22:6 "Start children off on the way they should go, and even when they are old, they will not turn from it."

Deuteronomy 6:6-7 "These commandments that I give you today are to be on your hearts. Impress them on your children. Talk about them when you sit at home and when you walk along the road, when you lie down and when you get up."

Proverbs 13:22 (NIV): "A good person leaves an inheritance for their children's children, but a sinner's wealth is stored up for the righteous."

If you take nothing else away from this book, understand that these principles are worth MASTERING!! Don't just learn them and use them here and there. Take the time and put forth the effort to master them. Knowledge without execution is just potential. The moment you start applying these principles, you shift from being controlled by money to controlling it. That's what God wants from us and for us in this area.

So, here's my charge to you: DON'T WAIT!!! Don't file this book away as "good ideas." Decide right now to put these principles into practice. Step into the driver's seat of your financial life, lead your family with confidence, and build a future that reflects your faith, not your fears.

You have the power! You have the tools! Now is the time to act! NOW IS THE TIME TO PROSPER!

Know that I'm rooting for you. I'm praying for you. I'm believing God for incredible testimonies of obedience to His word and financial freedom!

Meet the Author

Kirstie O'Banner is a wife, mother, and devoted follower of the Lord, Jesus Christ. She is passionate about helping others grow in their understanding of God's word and their relationship with Him. She lives a life of service, continually seeking ways to positively impact others for the glory of God.

Professionally, she is a real estate broker and owner of LivWell Realty, Inc., based in Orlando, FL. She is also a mortgage broker and real estate investor.

In 2015, Kirstie and her husband, Samuel, founded Fresh Start Financial Education LLC.

Together, they have coached many families from all over the country towards financial freedom. Their journey to debt freedom has inspired countless people worldwide. They host workshops, teach classes, and have an online course that can be found on their websites: www.FreshStartFreedom.com and www.TheFreshStartAcademy.com.

Resources

Visit:

www.KirstieOBanner.com

for valuable resources.

The Fresh Start Fast Track course
can be found at

www.FreshStartFreedom.com

or

www.TheFreshStartAcademy.com

Join the exclusive **Purposed To
Prosper - Community** Facebook
group for additional insight, advice,
and accountability.

Notes